WHAT'S WRONG WITH MY FAMILY?

GROWING UP IN AN ALCOHOLIC HOME

Magdaline DeSousa

The opinions expressed in this manuscript are solely the opinions of the author and do not represent the opinions or thoughts of the publisher. The author has represented and warranted full ownership and/or legal right to publish all the materials in this book.

What's Wrong With My Family? Growing Up in An Alcoholic Home

All rights reserved.

Copyright © 2022 by Magdaline DeSousa

Cover photo by Mary Burrows

No part of this book may be reproduced in any form or by any electronic or mechanical means, including information storage and retrieval systems, without written permission from the author, except for the use of brief quotations in a book review.

ISBN (paperback): 978-1-950306-25-1 (ebook): 978-1-950306-26-8

Library of Congress Catalog Number: 2020921901

Table of Contents

Acknowledgments		iii
Foreword		v
I.	Is This Normal?	1
II.	What Does it All Mean?	5
III.	Growing Up in an Alcoholic Home	13
IV.	Finally Free! Or Was I?	27
V.	How I Survived	33
VI.	Why Should You Get Help?	39
VII.	Where Can You Get Help?	49
VIII.	It Does Get Better	61
References		67

Acknowledgements

As always, I want to thank my friends and family for their endless support while I share my story to help others. I am honored to have you on this journey with me.

Foreword

When I first started writing this book, I envisioned myself as the audience. Magda, at various ages between 11 and 18, growing up in an alcoholic home—not knowing what it was, what was wrong, or what to do. I felt like I was dying inside.

After I finished this book, I now believe it is for anyone who is struggling with the family disease of alcoholism and is looking for answers. Anyone who wants to know more about it, how it affects them, and how they can get help. I pray my story gives you strength, hope, and healing from this cunning, baffling, and powerful disease.

1

Is This Normal?

Let's begin by talking about you. You bought this book because you have a feeling something isn't right, but you don't know what it is. Maybe you lie awake at night, asking yourself questions such as:

Is it normal that...?

1. Mom drinks so much every day, every weekend, every holiday
2. Dad rages and you never know what is going to happen
3. Dad gets drunk at the dinner table and passes out
4. You lie and cover for Mom—at school, at work, to your family and friends
5. You move around a lot
6. You worry where your next meal will come from or whether the bills will be paid
7. You already work to support your family at a young age
8. You tiptoe around the house because you never know what to expect (*Is Mom in a good mood? What's going to set Dad off this time?*)

9. None of your friends come over because you're afraid of what state Mom or Dad will be in
10. You cry all the time

You may not ask yourself these questions, but certain behaviors could indicate something is off. I always sensed from a young age I had to be a little adult. I was the responsible one because no one else was. Dad was busy drinking, and Mom was busy taking care of Dad and working to pay the bills. This left my younger brother John and me, so I took care of him. It was my job. A job I was not qualified for, didn't ask for, and shouldn't have been given at 10 years old.

Like me, you may be the responsible one in the house: the one who pays the bills, cooks dinner, and does all the household chores. The one who wakes Mom or Dad for work so they get there on time, with coffee and breakfast in hand. The one who calls in for him or her when they are too drunk to show up. You may also take care of yourself and any other children in the house by getting everyone ready for school, making sure homework is done, forms are signed, and all of you get to the bus on time.

I could go on and on, but the simple answer is no. None of this is normal. Moreover, it's not healthy. You should have a parent taking care of you, making sure you have food, shelter, and clothes. That you are ready to start your day and have what you need for school. However, just because these dynamics exist in your family doesn't mean you are living in an alcoholic home. I am not here to diagnose you or your family. I am only someone who lived through this and wants to share my experiences to benefit you. I'm not a licensed counselor or therapist. Even if I was, it's impossible to define what is going on without talking to you.

Fortunately, there are resources to help you determine if alcoholism is affecting your family (and yes, it affects the entire family). There are questionnaires you can take on the Al-Anon Family Group's website[1] to guide you.

What's Wrong With My Family?

Al-Anon is a support group for friends and families who are affected by someone's drinking. We'll talk more about Al-Anon later, but for now, I pulled a few questions from their online surveys for you to consider, in addition to the questions I listed above:

Are you <u>living</u> with a problem drinker?

1. Are mealtimes, birthdays, and holidays ruined because of drinking?
2. Do you make promises, such as *"I'll get better grades"* or *"I'll keep my room clean"* for the drinking and fighting to stop?
3. Are you scared to ride in the car with the drinker?
4. Have you considered calling the police because of abusive behavior?
5. Do you ever treat teachers, friends, teammates, etc. unfairly because you are angry?

Did you <u>grow up</u> with a problem drinker?

1. Do you constantly seek approval from others?
2. Have you had problems with your own compulsive behavior?
3. Do you feel more alive in the midst of crisis?
4. Do you care for others easily, yet find it difficult to care for yourself?
5. Do you attract and/or seek people who tend to be compulsive and/or abusive?
6. Do you often mistrust your own feelings and the feelings expressed by others?

If you answered *yes* to any of the questions in this chapter, you may be living with, or have grown up with, an alcoholic. The reality of this and what it means for you may take a long time to settle in. As a young child and teenager, I was so lost, scared, and confused. I had no idea what was going on. I was desperate for someone to talk to who could understand what I was feeling. Somebody who would tell me it was going to be okay. I am here to tell you now that someone understands. I know your pain. I know your hurt. I know your heart. And it will be okay...one day, it will be okay.

The good news is you took the first step by buying this book to find answers. Here, I will define what it means to be an alcoholic, how growing up in an alcoholic home impacted me (as a child, teenager, young adult, and adult), how I got help, and how my life has changed. I ask you to open your mind to what is in here. I wish I knew then what I know now. I could have saved myself years of pain. Try to think of me as the future you, coming back to tell you that you **can** reach your full potential: a life filled with joy and happiness *whether or not* the alcoholic in your life stops drinking.

Thoughts to Consider...

1. What made you want to buy or read this book?

2. Are there any questions or behaviors listed in this chapter that are familiar to you? If so, what are they?

3. What else, if anything, can you relate to so far?

II

What Does It All Mean?

As with most new things, there is a lot of terminology that can be confusing when you first start to learn. Before we go any further, let's define some of the basics.

What is an Alcoholic?

An alcoholic is someone who cannot control their drinking. Once they start, they have a hard time stopping. Oftentimes when they are drunk, damaging and scary things can happen. They may be abusive: emotionally, verbally, physically, and/or sexually. The alcoholic might fight with others at the slightest provocation, possibly leading to injury or arrest. Financial problems could exist, such as not being able to pay the rent or bills and being forced to move. Some families even experience homelessness.

The alcoholic typically blacks out and has no recollection of what they said or did, leaving those who do remember what happened feeling confused and invalidated. If alcoholics can't remember, they have no reason to apologize or change their behavior.

WHAT DOES IT ALL MEAN?

Even if someone only drinks once a year, blacks out, crashes the family car, and is arrested, this is still a sign of a problem.

You may have heard of Alcoholics Anonymous (AA), but you don't know exactly how it works. AA is an international group of people who have drinking problems, with meetings available almost everywhere worldwide. There are no age or education requirements. Anyone who wants to do something about their drinking problem can join. AA's primary book of literature, called the *Big Book*, sites medical research by Dr. William Silkworth (1939) which states people with drinking problems are allergic to alcohol. Once someone who is allergic has developed the habit, they can never safely use alcohol in any form again. Alcoholism is quite literally considered a disease[2].

This theory has been debated throughout the decades. Recent research from 2016 supports the concept that an alcoholic **does** physically and mentally respond to alcohol differently than a normal drinker. According to the National Institute on Alcohol Abuse and Alcoholism, *"alcohol use and alcohol-related problems are influenced by [the way in which alcohol is broken down by the body]."*

Whatever causes an alcoholic's body to react differently, once the craving for alcohol begins, they are helpless against it[3]. To date, the only known cure is to abstain from drinking, though mental health and research organizations continue to look for concrete solutions, such as medications. The main takeaway here is that once alcoholics start drinking, for whatever reason, they cannot control it.

AA has 12 questions an individual can answer to see if they qualify as an alcoholic. Perhaps you recognize your parent in some of these, or maybe he or she has expressed these thoughts to you at times:

1. Have you ever decided to stop drinking for a week, but only lasted for a couple of days?
2. Do you wish people would mind their own business about your drinking and stop telling you what to do?

3. Have you ever switched from one kind of drink to another in hopes this would keep you from getting drunk?
4. Have you had to have an eye-opener upon awakening during the past year? (An eye-opener is a drink to get your day started and/or stop the shaking.)
5. Do you envy people who can drink without getting into trouble?
6. Have you had problems connected with drinking during the past year?
7. Has your drinking caused trouble at home?
8. Do you ever try to get "extra" drinks at a party because you do not get enough?
9. Do you tell yourself you can stop drinking any time you want to, even though you keep getting drunk when you don't mean to?
10. Have you missed days of work or school because of drinking?
11. Do you have "blackouts"? (A "blackout" is when you have been drinking for hours or days which you cannot remember.)
12. Have you ever felt your life would be better if you did not drink?

Depending on the severity of the drinking, alcoholics who stop drinking may go into withdrawal. Alcoholism is a form of addiction and as with any substance abuse, withdrawal can be deadly without assistance. They might need to be admitted into a 28-day treatment center to get through "the shakes" and the cravings. Sadly, getting sober is only the first step. Without support, such as individual or group therapy, many alcoholics will return to drinking. Why is this? Alcohol is often used to numb some deeper pain the alcoholic is experiencing; alcoholism is only a symptom of the real problem. Once the alcoholic doesn't have their substance to block everything out, they must face their behaviors, including all they've done to their loved ones. Often it is too overwhelming, so they drink to cope.

If an alcoholic continues to drink, they get wet brain. Wet brain is a form of brain damage resulting from repeated and heavy exposure to alcohol. Alcohol limits the absorption of thiamine (vitamin B1)[4], decreasing the thiamine reserve stored in the liver. If a person continues to abuse alcohol, it creates a thiamine deficiency, which causes brain damage. This can result in confusion, memory loss, or physical paralysis, among other symptoms. It is a terrible thing to witness.

Even with support, the sustained sobriety rate remains low. In the Al-Anon meetings I attend, I have heard stories of alcoholics who were sober for 15-20 years and started drinking again. It is heartbreaking for those families to experience, and painful for them to watch someone they love suffer. I'm not telling you this to upset you; I'm telling you this so you can understand how powerful this disease is. I once heard it said alcoholism kills anything pure, kind, and loving. Don't underestimate its effect on you and your family.

What is an Al-Anon? A Codependent?

What does it mean to be a child of an alcoholic, an adult child, an Al-Anon, and/or codependent? Simply, a *child of an alcoholic* is a young person growing up with one or more alcoholic parents or caregivers. An *adult child* is an adult who grew up with one or more alcoholic parents or caregivers. An *Al-Anon* is anyone worried about someone with a drinking problem (spouse/partner, parent, child, sibling, aunt/uncle, friend, co-worker) and is affected by that person's drinking.

A family dealing with someone who has an alcohol abuse problem cannot function properly. A dysfunctional family is one in which all the attention and energy is focused on the alcoholic family member. This leads to codependence[5], which means putting someone else's needs, desires, emotions, and welfare before your own. Codependents usually sacrifice themselves at all costs, even their identity and safety, to take care of the alcoholic. They want so badly to believe things will get better that they do whatever the alcoholic asks, hoping he/she will change, and the drinking will stop. Unfortunately, alcoholics and addicts are charmers who are good at getting what they want. They will say or do whatever they need, make promises, and break them, to get their drug of choice.

Alcoholism, or any kind of substance abuse, is a family disease. In a dysfunctional family, everyone suffers from fear, anger, pain, shame, and codependent behaviors. But no one talks about anything, especially how they feel, what's going on, or what is happening with the alcoholic. The proverbial elephant in the room is ignored or worse, people just walk around it. Because of this, codependents learn to ignore their needs and block out their emotions. Growing up, I got in trouble when I was angry or upset, so eventually, I shut down as I got older. If you ever tried to express yourself, you likely had a similar experience, which reinforced your decision to stay quiet.

This coping mechanism may help you survive your traumatic environment, but it won't serve you later in life. It makes it hard to get in touch with *any* of your feelings, even the good ones. For example, it took me more than ten years in therapy to identify how I felt about a situation. Does it make me happy? Sad? Frustrated? Hopeful? Hopeless? Angry? It's only while writing this book that I allowed myself to feel grief and other emotions from my childhood. Interestingly, I learned in my counseling sessions that I didn't believe it was okay for me to be happy either, so I focused on the problems in my life rather than the positive things. I unconsciously sabotaged a lot of good situations and potential relationships because I didn't know how to live an uneventful, content life.

Growing up in an alcoholic family leaves deep, lasting wounds that can only be healed with awareness, therapy, and time. If these are not addressed, Al-Anons or people who are codependent may turn to substances themselves to cope with the pain and trauma. These individuals call themselves "double winners," those who are in multiple treatment programs. Studies show alcoholism is 50 percent connected to genetics (it can be passed down through your genes). If you have a family history of alcoholism, you have a higher risk of developing a drinking problem[6]. Either that, or you might find someone like your alcoholic parent to fill the void and continue the cycle of abuse, whether in a romantic relationship, a friendship, or in a professional relationship at work. It's not intentional; it's conditioning.

For you and your family to heal, everyone needs help. Fortunately, there are support groups for everyone affected by someone's drinking. We already discussed AA, which is for the alcoholic. Al-Anon is for friends and families of alcoholics. Alateen is a part of Al-Anon for young people ages 10-19 living with alcoholism, and Adult Children of Alcoholics / Dysfunctional Families (ACA) is for adult children of alcoholics who grew up in dysfunctional homes. I will discuss each of these more in Chapter 7.

Now that you have a better understanding of what all this terminology means, perhaps you identify with all or some of what I've shared so far. Maybe you're still not sure if your family is affected by alcoholism or are having trouble accepting it's true. What does it mean if everything is *not* okay and there's a problem no one is talking about? After all, they're your family; it's all you've ever known. I was there for a long time myself, but I can't say this enough: trust yourself.

We are all born with an inner wisdom, a navigation system of sorts. You may hear this referred to as your instinct, your gut, or simply "a feeling." When I first started trauma therapy, I was so confused. Where was this instinct everyone talked about? I certainly didn't have one. Finally, someone explained it to me as "a feeling in the pit of your stomach." When I heard that, I realized that I did have an instinct, but I had been taught not to listen to it.

Another way to think of it is this: your instinct is your first reaction to a situation. If you immediately feel good about a person or situation, your instinct is probably telling you that it's safe. If you hesitate or have a weird feeling, your gut may be telling you something is wrong. I have learned over the years to stop questioning myself.

Sometimes I don't even understand my instinct, or why something or someone feels off to me, but I'd rather be safe than sorry. Your gut is there—you're just not used to listening to it. The more you heal, the easier it gets to hear it. The bottom line is this: No one knows what is best for you, other than you! If you think or feel something is off, it probably is. Trust your instincts.

Thoughts to Consider...

1. When you read these definitions (alcoholic, Al-Anon, codependent), what parts of them can you identify in your parent/s, your family, or yourself?

2. Have you tried to talk about what's going on in your family? If so, what happened? If not, why haven't you?

3. Do you have things you want to say, but are afraid to speak up? What do you think might happen if you do?

Growing Up in An Alcoholic Home

AUTHOR'S NOTE:
My goal in writing this book is to share my story and help others, by keeping the focus on my journey. There are times where it may seem like details are missing, and this is intentional. Whatever I've been through in my relationships, I want to respect those individuals and their privacy. I hope you can understand and still benefit from my experiences.

To be honest, I don't remember much of my childhood. From the time I was 18 and younger, I can count roughly 40-50 memories, and sadly, most of them are not good. Fast-forward to my twenties and early thirties and the memories remain slim. This always bothered me. Why couldn't I remember things, especially my childhood? High school? College? My first job and all the international travels I worked so hard to afford?

Through years of therapy, Al-Anon, and other healing practices, I learned these memory lapses are a result of disassociation, which occurs in response to trauma. Trauma is defined as a deeply distressing or disturbing experience. Disassociating is how I disconnected from the emotional pain I felt in response to this *distressing and disturbing* home environment. This allowed me to survive by not being fully present in my body. While I don't have many actual memories, I do have feeling memories. I remember vividly what it felt like to live in an alcoholic home. And if I ever forget, one trip to visit my parents can remind me, depending on the day.

My father was more verbally abusive to us than physically abusive. My grandfather was also an alcoholic (who eventually quit drinking later in his life), and at times he was physically abusive to my father. Because of this, my father never drank at home and rarely hit us. I am thankful he tried to break this part of the cycle with us. However, looking back on it, the verbal abuse was severe. Some therapists argue verbal abuse is as bad, if not worse, than physical abuse. Physical wounds heal, but verbal abuse cuts to our soul, our psyche, and who we are. Those wounds can last a lifetime if they are not acknowledged, addressed, and treated.

By the time I was 18, we had moved roughly 25 times because of my dad. He either gambled the rent while he was drinking, lost his job and got a new one in another city or state, or was running away from something. At 10 years old, I became an expert at packing my room and I was proud of it. I don't even know how it happened. Now, it breaks my heart. I knew then something was wrong, but I wasn't sure what it was.

Although I don't remember much, I kept journals from the time I was 10-17. I couldn't read them for almost 20 years. I simply moved them with me from high school, to college, and from house to house, until one day, they ended up in storage. In my mid-thirties, as part of my therapy, I finally read them and cried for days. It's what inspired me to write this book…to help others like me. I want to share some of those entries with you now. If you aren't sure there is a problem with drinking in your home, you might relate to how I felt at certain times while growing up in an alcoholic home. This may help you figure out what's going on.

My Childhood

When I started journaling around 10 years old, my entries were mostly positive. I talk about how I love my family and feel lucky to have my parents. It was almost my dad's birthday and I was saving money to buy him a present. I missed him because he was working lots of late nights and I hadn't seen him in a few days. We were moving and I begged my dad to let me switch schools, but I didn't tell him why. For some reason, I didn't feel like I could tell either of my parents, but I was being bullied regularly at school, emotionally and physically.

I was made fun of for what I wore, what I looked like, who I liked, what I said, and who I was friends with. I was shoved into lockers, pushed down the stairs, and my books were knocked out of my hands, just to name a few instances. Even the teachers were mean to me. They didn't believe me when things happened, or made fun of me for getting offended. One time, I was beaten in gym class with the soccer ball and the gym teacher said to me, *"God, Maggie, you're always getting hurt."* You can imagine how upset and alone I felt as a young child.

> *"I feel like a rotten, unopened sack of potatoes that will soon be thrown away. I am really sad when people ignore me or act like they don't care."*

It makes me wonder...why didn't anyone notice what was going on? How come no one asked me questions about how I was feeling? Bullying wasn't given as much attention back then as it is today, so that may have been a large part of it. More likely, as I mentioned earlier, in dysfunctional families, all the attention goes to the person who is an alcoholic or addict. How *could* anyone see what was going on with me? Whatever the reason, if you are being bullied, try to find someone who can advocate for you, in or outside of your family. No one, even a teacher, has the right to make you feel like garbage.

When I turned 11, there were some entries about my dad and mom, me being upset, and my dad yelling at my mom. Again, I focused mostly on the bullying at school. A few months after I turned 11, I started to recognize what was going on in our home. How did I go from loving my family and feeling lucky to have them to living in the endless hell I remember? My therapist explained to me that somewhere around ages 11-12, children start to experience reality differently. This is normal as you mature and become more aware of your surroundings. It's painful to go from loving your family to *"Oh my God—what is happening?"* If you feel this way and can't understand what's changed in your family, you are not alone.

For me, I began to notice the broken promises from my dad, the lying, and my mother's mental stress. One day my mom and dad were nice to me, the next they were mean or yelling. My brother was an angry child and started taking it out on me, but no one seemed to believe me. Confused is the best word to describe me at this age.

> *"I have a pretty funny, caring, hitting, hurting, kind of family and it gets confusing. I love them (I think I do) but I'm not sure they always want me."*

I had nowhere to put my feelings and when I tried, I got in trouble. So, I hid how I felt most of the time. I hid what was going on at school. I hid how badly I was hurt by my brother. I hid everything. The only place I ever let anything out was in my journal. This is when I first started getting sick with headaches, stomachaches, tonsillitis, and bronchitis. Anyone impacted by someone's drinking, such as children of alcoholics, adult children, or Al-Anons, often have health issues related to the stress of living in such an environment. When emotions are held inside, they begin to impact your physical and mental well-being. You must learn to let them out; if not, they will find a way to express themselves.

My feelings of being unloved intensified as the months of being 11 went by. There was always something going on, at home or in school. I don't remember being a kid and playing without a care in the world. It seems I had few moments where I was purely happy. I'm sure there were some—not every day could have been awful. However, all I could see was the pain, which got worse as the disease progressed. Month after month, my journal entries became more depressed and unstable.

> *"I feel mad, embarrassed, scared, alone, unloved, and unwanted. I feel like I'd be better off dead. I feel a couple more things I can't explain. It's like my heart is breaking into a thousand pieces."*

I thought a lot about suicide; it seemed like the only way out. Thankfully, by the time I was 14, I realized it was a permanent solution to a temporary problem. As I got older, I focused on getting out of the house and making a life for myself. But it was hard getting from day to day. I still didn't write about my dad's drinking; I don't think I noticed it. This is how alcoholism affects children. They are often confused, with big feelings it's hard for them (or you) to explain.

> *"I feel so sad I'm treated this way, and unloved because my mom, dad, and brother keep yelling at me. I'm lonely because no one knows I'm here. Mom says, "I love you. Your dad loves you. Your brother loves you, too." Do they? I guess I love them and maybe they love me. Do you suppose they treat me this way because they love me? I wonder..."*

First, how devastating that a child should question whether she is loved or wanted in her family. Whatever mistakes I make with my child (because we all make mistakes), I hope she never questions my love for her. I love my daughter exactly as she is, for who she is. Nothing she can do will change this. Second, how tragic that at such an early age, I associated abuse with love. *'Maybe their yelling at me means they love me?'* No wonder I found the unhealthy relationships I did later in my life. If this is you now, please know love is not abuse, verbal or physical. Love has no conditions. Love just is, and we all inherently deserve to be loved.

By age 12, I was the scapegoat of the family, the one everyone took their aggression out on. In a dysfunctional home, someone is usually targeted. My brother was frequently taking his anger out on me and then apologizing. My dad yelled at me for needing money for school projects and blamed me for things my brother did. My mother started taking *her* frustration and stress out on me. She also began telling me about her relationship problems, financial challenges, and other things going on in our home. Where else would it go? My dad was taking everything out on her, and she could barely function herself, let alone be present as a mother. (This behavior is common of the non-alcoholic parent in alcoholic households and confusing for children, but it is not healthy or normal.)

In addition to his drinking, my dad was strict, especially because I am a girl. This added another layer of difficulty to my childhood. On top of already feeling left out at home and in school, my dad's restrictions only made it worse. I wasn't allowed to do a lot of the things other kids my age could do, so I had trouble making friends. This also made me a target for further bullying. I felt even more hopeless and stayed up late, journaling at midnight, one, or two in the morning because I couldn't sleep.

"It's one thing to be treated like nothing, think you're nothing, but it's another to know you're nothing (which is what I am). I don't care about anything anymore. One of these days, I'm going to run away. That'll show them! Would they even care if I was gone?"

There were a lot of times I planned to run away, especially around this age. I packed my bags and knew which friend I would stay with (or the town I would go to). There was one problem…I couldn't leave my brother. I felt responsible for him. I was afraid of what might happen if I wasn't there to protect him. Despite everything, I loved John deeply. We held onto each other when everything was crazy in the storm of alcoholism. Although we had a contentious childhood, once I left for college, we became close. We realized how much we cared for each other and developed a loving relationship. In many ways, he gave me a purpose in life. He gave me a reason to stay. I can't imagine what life would have been like as a runaway.

When I read my journal entries now, I wonder how I made it through those years at all. In hindsight, I used school as a distraction from what was going on at home. Thankfully, I excelled there. I was recognized for my creativity and put into a gifted and talented program. I was on the Honor Roll and won multiple awards for various school projects. What a blessing it was that I had a healthy escape that served me later in life.

At age 13, I wrote about our financial struggles and moving a lot. I was happy when my dad got a job and we could pay the rent, but then we moved again. It was a part of life now. I needed glasses and my dad bought me an expensive pair that I wanted, which I appreciated. I was confused because my parents were still nice to me on some days and mean to me on others. I was getting sick more frequently, likely because of the increased stress.

However, I focused mostly on the continued drama at school. I obsessed over the popular girls and how to get them to like me, or how to find a boyfriend. This is a constant theme in my writing. When I first read my journals, I thought it was unusual to be so caught up in getting a boyfriend, especially at such an early age. In looking through them while writing this book, I realized I was desperate to be loved...to be accepted for who I was...to be seen by someone, anyone. No one should feel this way, but many people do, even as adults.

When I got closer to turning 14, I experienced rage episodes I didn't understand, during which I didn't feel like myself. One time, I closed the door to my room, blasted Guns and Roses, and threw things everywhere. Then, I calmly cleaned up, put everything back, and went on with my day as if nothing happened.

"What am I going to do? I'm going crazy. I snapped and I have a feeling I will snap again. I can't take all this misery, nosiness, craziness, and torture! It is hell here. No one seems to want to help me or care. I've thought about killing myself, but I don't think I would actually do it. As bad as it is, I want to survive and get out of here. To be on my own, as far away as possible."

Somehow, I continued to do well in school, which was a lifesaver for me and likely hid some of what was really going on at home. This reflected later in my life as well. Whatever was going on personally, I always did well professionally. On the outside, I looked like I had it together. How could anyone know something was wrong?

The High School Years

The summer before high school, we moved again, and I started freshman year in a new district. I took this opportunity to start over and fit in. I bought clothes everyone wore and styled my hair so no one could make fun of me. Overall, it worked, and my high school years were socially the best years of my education. However, it was dreadful at home. The abuse got worse with my parents, but at least my brother stopped taking his anger out on me as much.

I felt like a second-class citizen, a slave doing all the chores, even if I was sick. My stomach issues and headaches got worse. Additionally, I developed vertigo. I would get dizzy and black out in random places, at home and at school. But my dad thought I was lying to get out of something. I wrote a poem called "Trapped" right before my fourteenth birthday:

In a cage is where I stay
Keeping my fear and anger locked away
One day I hope to be free
To find a way out
To find the key
I've had times of madness

What's Wrong With My Family?

I've had feelings of sadness
I wish someone could see
And have the heart to let me be
In a cage is where I say
I wonder if I'll be here till I wither away
I'm dying inside
Can't anyone see?
Won't somebody please release me?

In response to the continued stress, my behavior started to change in multiple ways. I was mean and disrespectful to everyone: my teachers, my friends, my grandmother, and my mother. One of the Alateen questions is: *Do you ever treat teachers, friends, teammates, etc. unfairly because you are angry about someone's drinking?*

Looking back, I can see I started taking my aggression out on others, like my family was doing with me. Where else would it go? Although I didn't understand what was going on, I did eventually realize my behavior was unacceptable. I felt so ashamed. I wrote a note to my teachers and friends, apologizing and vowing to do better. I apologized to my grandmother and started treating her better. Even though my mother and I had a touchy relationship, I attempted to be nicer to her, too.

I tried drinking to see if I would feel better, but I only drank occasionally and never got drunk. I considered cutting and hurting myself. I understand now this was in response to the pain I was feeling…a way to try to release it.

> *"I keep wondering what it would be like to have a knife go through my leg or arm. I know I could never do it, but it bothers me to have these thoughts."*

I was tired all the time, but I couldn't sleep. I felt so anxious, isolated, and abused. I had one good friend at the time who I felt safe confiding in. She was concerned about me and talked to her counselor about my situation. Her counselor said to get help and gave her two anonymous hotline numbers for me. I was scared, but I eventually called. I thank God for whoever was on the other end of the line and listened to me. They saved my life.

By sophomore year, school was going well socially. I finally made some good friends. I was with people who were smart like me, so I fit in. My teachers noticed my writing skills and other areas of academic strength. I enrolled in college-level courses and joined activities I enjoyed, including: musical theatre, chorus, Future Business Leaders of America, and the school newspaper. I had no encouragement at home and had to fight to be involved in each of these, which made things worse. Yet again, I felt alone, abandoned, and not recognized for all my accomplishments.

"I do everything I can to try to fill another's shoes, but I'm not someone else. I'm me. I'm afraid if I am me, no one will like me. I feel out of place and lost. No one loves me, no one wants me. Where do I go? Where do I fit in?"

I wasn't allowed to date, but I did have a couple of boyfriends anyway. Sadly, those guys wanted only one thing and when I didn't give it, they left. Meanwhile, the good guys didn't come near me because of my father. Who would ever date someone that came from my background? I felt rejected and it validated my feelings of worthlessness.

Such petty problems in such a big life
So much for one to do alone
Alone...alone...alone is where I am
No one to help me.
I'm going out of my mind
Looking for something I can't find
I can only ask one question, why?
All I want to do is die.

A month later, I revised my journal to say life is a blessing, no matter how painful it gets. *'You have to look on the bright side, if you can find one. We are all here for a reason.'* Unfortunately, this didn't last long.

> *"I feel disassociated and detached from everyone—family, friends, school, life. I've never been depressed for this long before. Everywhere I go, I feel unimportant and trivial. No one gives a crap. I don't understand it. I feel like I'm going to have a nervous breakdown. I just want to sleep and forget it all."*

As an adult, I learned mental health is affected not only by genetics but also by the environments we live in. Growing up in an addictive or abusive household can cause members of the family to experience mental health challenges. I believe my journal entries indicate early signs of depression or something deeper, although none of us knew it then. If you can relate to this, there might be something health-related that counseling and/or medication can help.

Junior year should have been great for me. School continued to go well. I got the lead in the school play and my teachers and friends supported me. I was now the editor of the school paper and successful in my other activities. I got my driver's license and could drive my mother's car, so I had some freedom (at my father's discretion). I had a job. I was closer to getting out of the house, to being free, but different things were coming up. I was worried I wouldn't be able to make it to the end. My father continued to disapprove of my participation in extracurricular activities, but I knew it was important for me to get into college, so we argued constantly. I didn't journal much this year, probably because I was busy. However, I wrote one entry the summer after junior year:

> *"This year has been absolute hell. I thought it would never end! I can't believe it has. I'm a senior! In one year, I go to college. I'll finally be out of this house and on my own. I'm a little scared, but I'm so relieved."*

Senior year, my parents decided to move *again*, an hour and a half away. I insisted on staying to finish high school. I was established in my school and concerned about doing well to get into college. I told the district superintendent about my situation and he authorized me to do whatever I needed to stay there. What a blessing he was!

My best friend's parents let me live with them during the week so I could attend high school. It was a beautiful home and I had my own bathroom downstairs. I slept on a pullout couch in the office and I was so incredibly grateful to be there. Dinner was every night at the same time, and mealtimes were uneventful and normal. My friend's mother helped me with my school projects and talked to me about colleges. I'd never experienced that before. I had chores, like cleaning the table and loading the dishwasher, but I wanted to do them. It was the least I could do to express my gratitude for being there.

Overall, it was the most peaceful time of my teenage years. I had to drive home every weekend, and there was still drama and alcoholic moments, but at least I had a break and some distance from the craziness during the week. It was truly a moment of grace and I will never forget my friend's family for giving me a safe space with some sense of stability and normalcy.

This marks the end of my young adult journey. I didn't share these thoughts to upset you, but if you have any of the same ones, hopefully this gives you hope that you can make it one day, too. Maybe your situation is better than mine, maybe it's worse, or maybe it's just different. This is not about measuring the level of abuse. Abuse is abuse, and no child should suffer through it.

The good news is I no longer think of my life as I once did, and I feel truly blessed I made it here. I reflect on where I am today emotionally, mentally, and spiritually in my closing chapter. But first, on to college.

Thoughts to Consider...

1. Have you ever thought about or tried to hurt yourself? If yes, what thoughts and feelings are taking you to this place?

2. Do you feel depressed, tired all the time, or suffer from other health issues? If so, what do you think could be causing this?

3. Have you tried to talk to anyone about your feelings, but no one understands? If so, how does this make you feel?

4. Can you relate to any of the feelings I experienced as a young adult and teenager? If so, which ones and why?

5. Take some time to write down your feelings and thoughts. This is a safe space for you to let it all out and honor yourself.

IV

Finally Free! Or Was I...?

From as early as I can remember, I planned my escape from that house, and that escape was college. Because of my academics and extracurricular activities, I got a few small scholarships and qualified for student loans. I attended a university out-of-state, roughly six hours away from home—just far enough. I was so excited. I knew everything was going to be okay. Better than okay, it would be great!

And...it wasn't.

On To College

The summer before I left for college, I met an older man. I was 18 and he was 24. We started dating and fell in love quickly. Suddenly, I didn't want to leave anymore, but I had to. We decided to date long distance and figure out a way to make it work. I spent a good amount of my freshman year driving back and forth between New York and Virginia to visit him (or he visited me on weekends). He was verbally abusive, and we had explosive fights, but I didn't think much of it. Although it upset me, I was used to it; it's how I grew up.

I missed him terribly and hated being away at school. What the hell was going on? I worked so hard to get to this point in my life, and now I wasn't enjoying it.

I took my first semester of sophomore year off. I considered transferring to a college in New York to be closer to my boyfriend. We ended up living together and it didn't go well. Ultimately, I decided to return to school in Virginia after winter break, but we continued to date. My second semester of sophomore year, things went downhill once I got back. I can't remember exactly what triggered it, but depression overtook me. No one really knew what was going on. Growing up in an alcoholic home, I learned to be good at hiding my emotions. For three weeks, I only left my dorm room to get food. I didn't want to do anything. What was wrong? I was supposed to be HAPPY. I was out of the house, on my own, and away from my parents. Why couldn't I get out of bed?

Fortunately, I realized something wasn't right and I went to my school's counseling center. This began my healing journey. They did an intake and asked me questions to determine if I needed services. I was diagnosed with depression and anxiety and assigned a therapist. I never had a professional to talk to before (other than the hotlines I called). I shared my story and told the therapist everything that was going on. He introduced me to the concept of alcoholism and recommended regular counseling sessions. He also suggested I attend an Adult Children of Alcoholics (ACOA) meeting on campus.

When I first started going to meetings, I went to ACOA meetings. At the time, ACOA was only for adult children of alcoholics. ACOA eventually evolved into ACA, Adult Children of Alcoholics/Dysfunctional Families, and is now a program for children who grew up in any type of dysfunctional home.

I'll never forget my first ACOA meeting. As I listened to everyone share, I realized they were telling my stories. I wasn't crazy. I wasn't alone. There was something wrong and it had nothing to do with me. I was so relieved. I attended ACA for a semester and went to a couple of Al-Anon meetings whenever I was home in New York. I figured it was good enough. *'Why do I need to go anymore? I know it's a problem, I know it's not in my head, and I have a therapist.'*

Meanwhile, the verbal abuse escalated in my relationship. My college roommates held an intervention because they believed my boyfriend was hitting me from the fights they heard. I was shocked—of course he wasn't! However, when I presented the situation to my therapist, he agreed with my roommates and expressed his concern, as well. In hindsight, what was I doing? I tried to get out of the chaos of my home, and instead, I took it with me. I ended that relationship during my junior year of college, but I stayed in touch with him for roughly a year until I met someone new. I didn't know how to be alone, but I had some time before I realized this.

Life as an Adult Child

I graduated from college with honors, I ended the abusive relationship, I was in therapy, and I found a good job. Once again, I figured this was it. I was finally about to live the life I had dreamed of as a child. But what I learned in my alcoholic home lived on in my head. How could I be free with a mind programmed to doubt, put myself down, and not trust my instincts? It followed me everywhere.

I was also codependent, but I didn't know it yet. I had an extremely difficult time understanding my needs, let alone expressing them. I learned I had no voice because nothing I said mattered. Nothing I felt mattered. Nothing I thought or wanted mattered. I learned I didn't deserve to be respected, protected, or loved. I didn't deserve anything. I learned it was my job to take care of everybody else, so I put their needs before mine. I unconsciously picked relationships, friendships, and professional connections who used me or treated me badly, like I was treated in my family.

I believed my body defined me. I didn't feel I had a right to say no. I thought if I gave it, I would find someone to love me. The men I continued to date were all controlling, abusive, or had some sort of addiction. This put me in compromising positions, and I was date raped by a friend of a friend when I was 25. I got pregnant and had an abortion. It was the hardest decision of my life, but I knew I couldn't raise a child.

While this was terrible, I can't imagine how much worse it could have been. I coped with life's challenges by drinking and oftentimes blacking out, without fully comprehending what might have happened to me. I could be dead—or worse, I could have hurt someone with my irresponsible behavior. I am grateful to God for watching over me and keeping me alive during those years.

I ended up moving a lot, trying to figure out what I wanted to do with my life. Some of this is normal development, but it felt haphazard at times. When I was 25, I moved back to my college town to get my master's degree. I was a full-time graduate student and working a full-time *and* part-time job (60-70 hours a week. It was too much and I had a panic attack. My doctor recommended medication to ensure it didn't happen again, and I agreed. Interestingly, my depression felt better (even though my first therapist thought I didn't need medication. This started my medication journey for the next ten years. While it worked at times, I ultimately needed further intervention in my thirties.

Once I established a career, I threw myself into it. I worked 50-60 hours a week because the perfectionist in me could never leave a task undone. This was the first place I received validation as an adult, so I didn't want to let anyone down. I didn't want to fail. After all, I was only good enough if *(fill in the blank with any number of options)*. I was successful at work, well-dressed, good in bed, thin enough, made a lot of money, gave people money, gave people my time, etc. I wanted to make the outside perfect so the inside felt worthy.

Most people thought I had it together, and on the outside, I did, but not inside. I didn't realize this family disease set forth a pattern in my life that I would repeat over and over. I didn't realize I was conditioned to live in chaos. Normal didn't feel normal to me; sometimes it still doesn't. Whenever things started to calm down, I unconsciously did something to disrupt my life. I got into a tremendous amount of debt, resumed risky behaviors, or found another dysfunctional partner who abused me—anything to feel at home. I didn't understand until much later what was happening.

In my late twenties, I met my now ex-husband. I told myself I would never marry someone like my father, and I didn't—not exactly. He had a full-time job with benefits, came from a loving, stable family, and was smart and charming. Unfortunately, there were some unhealthy similarities.

I got married with nearly ten years of therapy and eight years of Al-Anon under my belt (though I was not active in Al-Anon at the time. What upsets me the most is the person I became in my marriage. I lost myself because I was so focused on what he was doing all the time. This is what codependency can do to you.

Once I became a mother, I realized I was repeating my childhood, but in a different way. My Al-Anonism (as we say) followed me. There are many unhealthy behaviors you can learn growing up in alcoholism, and those came out with him. I knew things had to change, especially for my daughter. If your first motivation to get help is not for yourself, that's okay. Perhaps your motivation is for someone or something else. It's a good place to start. Eventually, it will become for you as well, and you will feel stronger and more empowered each day.

Thoughts to Consider...

1. When reading about my experiences as an adult, how does it make you feel to consider they are a result of growing up in an alcoholic home?

2. If you are a young adult, do you believe the family disease of alcoholism can affect you as an adult? Why or why not?

3. Have you ever considered that some of your challenges may be connected to growing up with alcoholism? If so, how does this make you feel?

4. If you are already an adult, what parallels can you make to what I've shared so far?

V
How I Survived

With those unbearable childhood years, lost, alone, and depressed, my confusing college years, chaotic 20s, and into a marriage where I repeated childhood patterns, you may be wondering—how did I survive? Resilience. This inner strength God gave me to bounce back in the face of adversity—to persevere and never give up. I believe you have it in you too, especially if you are reading this right now. What this tells me is you can make it, just like I did. My resilience drove me to get help, which gave me hope. How I got help evolved as I got older, but there were a variety of ways I reached out.

There were small ways I found comfort and forgot my troubles. These were things I could do at home or in my room, where I didn't feel afraid. I loved to read. I lost myself for hours in those stories, hoping I would be the heroine one day. I listened to music and found songs that reflected my thoughts, sometimes on repeat. I spent time in nature—I went for long bike rides, sat in a park, or played on the swings. Whenever I was outside, I felt free. The more you can get out of the house, the better.

Obviously, I wrote a lot. I would take my journal, find a space under a beautiful tree, and write. My journal was the safest space I had, where I could let out my deepest thoughts, without fear of getting in trouble. I wrote to God and prayed for Him to save me. I hid my journals, in ways I thought were clever, so my parents wouldn't find them and yell at me. My parents never did find them, so either I *was* clever or there was some divine intervention. Whatever the reason, I am grateful my space was respected. If you are a writer or feel inclined to write, this is something you can do to validate yourself and your feelings. Write about your experiences to see them in black and white, and say to yourself, *'This is really happening. I'm not crazy. This hurts me.'* (Or whatever other feelings come up.)

Then there were the big ways I reached out. The harder ones. The hardest one was talking to people. Who did I talk to? When I was younger, it started with one good friend I could trust. This led to an anonymous person on the end of a helpline. Once I got into high school, one of my teachers sensed what was going on. After she talked to me a few times, I knew she understood, so I confided in her. I also had a wonderful guidance counselor who helped me apply for college—and gave me an ear when I needed it. I was careful about what I shared because I was scared someone might report us to Social Services, but it was a comfort to be heard and treated with compassion.

I thank God for the phenomenal teachers who not only listened to me but also saw something in me and recommended I get involved in relevant after-school activities. My music teacher encouraged me in chorus and musical theatre. Singing is something I am good at, and those were two huge outlets for me. My accounting teacher urged me to sign up for Future Business Leaders of America and sponsored me to go to state finals. My English teacher persuaded me to join the school newspaper, where I eventually became the Editor-in-Chief. Each of these accomplishments boosted my self-confidence and I started to believe in myself, just a little bit.

As I got older, I made more friends I could trust—safe spaces to go when everything was hitting the fan. I went to support groups like ACA and Al-Anon and got additional encouragement from group members. I continued to learn more about alcoholism and how it affected me. In college, I found my first counselor, or therapist, and I still attend counseling today (although with a different therapist). I love having a place where I can talk about anything without judgment. My therapist is someone who can give me professional insights i nto what is going on with me and help me deal with any complex issues related to post-traumatic growth and healing.

Most importantly, I prayed. I believed in something greater than myself, which to this day, I identify as God. I know this can be a touchy subject for some of you, especially if you were not raised in religion or if you were raised to believe that religion is taboo. However, I wouldn't be true to my story if I didn't speak about this. When I read my journals for the first time, I believe the reason I am here is because of God. I wasn't alone; He was with me the entire time. My faith is stronger than ever because I have seen miracle after miracle He performs, including giving me my beautiful child.

If you don't believe in God, try to find something bigger than yourself, anything that can give you hope. In Al-Anon, we call this a higher power. Your higher power can be Allah, Buddha, the universe, spirit, nature, etc. For example, if your higher power is nature, you can take a walk or play outside. You may feel peaceful listening to the ocean waves or a babbling brook. Turn to that. Hold onto it. You don't have to talk about it with anyone; it's something just for you to get through life.

If you already believe in God, trust Him. Ask Him (or Her, or Them) for guidance. While it's hard to see during the storm, there is a reason you were born. You are here because you have a purpose to fulfill. Who knows where life will take you if you let it? I'm sorry if your parents can't see what an amazingly strong, brilliant, kind, caring, loving individual you are, but I can—and God can.

I love listening to online sermons, especially Pastor Joel Osteen. One of the things he says is:

"You came through your parents, but you are not of them. You are a child of God. If you believe in Him, he can take you places you've never dreamed."

This is but a season of life. With faith and prayer, you will get blessings back tenfold for all you're going through now. How could you not? God created you to have a wonderful life; I am living proof.

You might ask (which many people do, myself included) that if God loves you, why is He letting you go through this? This is a hard one for me to answer, even as a Christian who has seen miracles performed. However, I heard a sermon recently where Pastor Osteen said, *"Sometimes God challenges you so you can help others."* I think "challenge" is a bit of a light word for what some of us are going through, but the message to me is this: sometimes our struggles guide us to our purpose. I knew from the time I was nine years old I wanted to be an author. I dreamed of writing fairy tales or mystery novels. I never thought I would be a self-help and children's book author, but here I am. While I was composing this book, I realized all my writing has a common theme: awareness, education, and support.

I don't talk about this much because I have a separate book on it, but I lost my brother John to suicide during my senior year of college. *The Forgotten Mourners: Sibling Survivors of Suicide* is the first book I wrote for sibling survivors of suicide (and how I endured his loss). I cannot tell you how many people have reached out to me, grateful for someone who can relate. I have also had people tell me my book saved their lives. Once they read it, they realized what it would do to their family if they completed suicide. If John's death and my pain can save and/or comfort others, our lives have meaning.

While this journey of growing up in an alcoholic household nearly broke me, it didn't. Now, I can share my story so someone like you can find a way to heal from this family disease and live a happy life.

If I can help one person by sharing this story, one little Magda, then my journey is worth it. This is my purpose. I know it's hard to believe, but I am grateful for both the challenges God gave me *and* the gift to share them.

There is a song I learned in high school chorus which seems fitting to end with here. It's called "To Everything There is a Season," by Ed Harris[7].

To everything there is a season,
To everything there is a time;
To every purpose under heaven
There is a time, a proper time.

A time to cast away
to bring together,
A time to be embraced,
to be alone;
To find and lose,
to keep and give,
There is a time, there is a time.

Thoughts to Consider:
1. What are a few small things you can do to find peace, both in and outside of your home?

2. Who can you talk to that may be able to understand your situation and/or help you figure out what to do?

3. Think about your gifts and talents. What do you love to do, or are good at? How can you use it as an outlet?

4. Do you have a "higher power" you turn to that gets you through the day?

   If so, what is it and how does it inspire you?

   If not, what could you incorporate from the suggestions above?

VI

Why Should You Get Help?

Why do you need to get help? Perhaps you think as I did—if you get out of the house, everything will be fine. Here's the problem: Growing up in alcoholism affects your ability to function in everyday life, regardless of whether you still live with the alcoholic or they continue to drink. If you don't address the unhealthy behaviors you learned in that environment, you will repeat the same dysfunctional patterns as an adult. I want to share one of the most powerful things I learned in Al-Anon. If you hear nothing else, please hear this:

Wherever you go, you take yourself with you.

I know people who moved across the country or overseas to get away from their families, only to find they were more miserable and self-destructive. It was like they never left home. Why is this? Dysfunction and chaos feel comfortable to us because it's all we've known our entire lives. Unconsciously, we look for people who remind us of our families. This feels safe because it's familiar, but it continues the toxic cycle of the family disease.

WHY SHOULD YOU GET HELP?

Learning to Set Boundaries

What are some unhealthy behaviors that can continue after you've left the house? You may still feel responsible for taking care of your family and put their needs before yours. This is my experience and the experience of countless others in Al-Anon. When I graduated from college and got a full-time job, I was so happy and proud of myself for achieving this milestone. Then, my parents started asking me for money. It didn't matter that I had rent to pay, a car payment, student loans, and other expenses. What were they going to do? Where would they go if I didn't pay their rent? At least I had a good job; they had nothing. I felt guilty, so I gave it to them.

You may find yourself in unhealthy, compromising situations like these as an adult because you never learned how to set boundaries. Boundaries are a critical part of taking care of yourself. They help you say no. More importantly, boundaries help you determine *when* to say no. Unfortunately, they rarely exist in most dysfunctional families, especially those struggling with alcoholism. You probably don't know how to say no or even if you try, it is not respected or heard in your home. How do you say no when you are taught to do whatever someone tells you? When you have no rights to your voice, your feelings, your money, your time, or even your body?

This is where boundaries come in. What exactly is a boundary? Boundaries are guidelines for you to feel safe and secure, physically, emotionally, mentally, and spiritually. They involve your beliefs, feelings, intuitions, and self-esteem. Boundaries protect you. They are not meant to keep people out; they allow people *safely* into your life. If someone violates a boundary, there is usually a clear consequence. If they continue to violate it, even after a consequence is imposed, you must decide if you want to keep that person in your life.

Here are a few examples:

- **Physical boundary:** No one touches you without your permission.
- **Consequence:** If they do, you will leave the situation and/or report them.

- **Emotional boundary:** No one tells you what or how to feel—you are true to your feelings and emotions. This doesn't mean someone has to agree with you, but they do have to respect your feelings.
- **Consequence:** You can avoid people who try to do this or not engage with them. You can also say things like, *"I guess we have to agree to disagree"* and change the topic.

- **Mental boundary:** No one can put you down, call you names, or make you feel worthless.
- **Consequence:** If they do, you will walk out of the room or end the conversation. In time, you may not allow this person in your life (this will be easier to do as you get older).

- **Spiritual boundary:** No one tells you who or what to believe in.
- **Consequence:** Again, you can avoid people who try to do this or not engage with them. You can also say things like, *"I guess we have to agree to disagree"* and change the topic.

Boundaries can be scary and confusing to enforce, especially when you are raised in an environment where no one has any. Al-Anon has some great tools on setting boundaries, which I've included along with other resources in Chapter 7, but this is where having professional guidance is valuable.

WHY SHOULD YOU GET HELP?

Most of the challenges I faced as an adult occurred because I had no boundaries. I allowed the wrong people and situations into my life. I did years of deep emotional work with trusted therapists, trauma and support groups, and energy workers to heal this dynamic, learn to take care of myself, and say no. Today, I know I am not responsible for taking care of anyone other than myself and my child. I never was. It takes time, patience, and persistence to get used to enforcing boundaries, but the more you do it, the easier it gets. And trust me, it's worth it!

Dealing with Your Family

Dealing with your family doesn't end once you leave the house. You may still interact with them at family functions, holidays, or other events. One day, you may have to decide: Do you stay in touch with your family? If so, how much and how often? Depending on the level of alcoholism, physical and emotional abuse, financial stress, etc., only you can make that choice. It is a personal decision and a difficult one. However, with the right support (Al-Anon, Alateen, individual therapy), you can do whatever is best for you. For me, I chose to keep my parents in my life.

You may also find yourself angry at whichever parent is not an alcoholic. You get this concept with the alcoholic (okay, fine it's a disease), but why isn't your *other parent* doing anything? There's nothing wrong with *them*. For me, it is my mother. I was angry with her for a long time. Why didn't she say anything? Why didn't she get us out of there? Why did she allow us to live like that? As a child, I often wished my mother would have divorced my father and left him. I figured if he were out of the picture, we would be fine. However, she never did. When I heard others share at meetings about being angry with their mothers and wishing the same things, I felt so much better for having these thoughts. I wasn't alone!

My Al-Anon sponsor once told me, *"Your mother is crippled emotionally. It's as if she is in a wheelchair and you keep asking her to walk. She can't."* After years of Al-Anon and individual therapy, I had to accept that my mother is also sick. Remember, we are **all** affected by the family disease of alcoholism. I tried for years to convince her to go to Al-Anon so she could see how this has affected her and get better. But she refused. She finally admitted she didn't want to get help. I imagine dealing with the truth of the situation is too overwhelming for her.

After the birth of my child, I had a hard time being fully present as a mother because I was so focused on my ex-husband. This is exactly what your parents are experiencing. Whoever the alcoholic is, the other parent is trying to control or fix them. It's all they know how to do to get through this and make things better. I finally found some compassion for my mother. Becoming a mother also made me realize something fundamental is missing in my parents. There is an Al-Anon slogan that says, *"Don't go to the hardware store looking for bread."* I know it's hard to accept or understand, but your mother and father are probably not capable of being parents—not without help. They love you, but they are sick and struggling.

On some level, this is freeing to me. It means it wasn't about me. It's about their diseases, their crippling diseases that prevent them from being healthy, loving, present parents. I wasn't a bad child or an ungrateful daughter; they just couldn't give me what I needed. They still can't. They do the best they can with what they have, and some days, that's enough for me. *"Progress, not perfection,"* as they say in Al-Anon. Other days, I turn elsewhere for what I need: friends, other family members, therapists, my healers, and God.

What if I'm Afraid to Get Help?

Getting help is essential but can be difficult or frightening depending on your situation. *What if I get in trouble?* You may risk further abuse or backlash from your family. Before I published this book, my father never knew I'd been in Al-Anon or individual/trauma counseling for nearly 20 years. He didn't know I'd reached out various times in my life, including in high school. Despite my fear, I knew it was time to speak my truth and share my story. Despite my fear as a teenager, I knew I had to talk to someone to survive. I encourage you to do the same. Find a person who you feel is safe and can keep your confidence.

Maybe you think like I did, *"If I get help, everyone will know, and no one can know. NO ONE can know what's going on."* This was our family mantra. Ironically, here is what I found out 15-20 years later—everyone knew. Everyone knew but me. My dad's behavior was erratic and violent at times. There were public, embarrassing moments in school and in our apartment complex. People may have said something to me, but if they did, I couldn't hear it. Because they knew, a few families adopted me as a third daughter, and I will forever be grateful to them, whether we remain in touch today. They gave me a safe place to go when I needed one.

In my mid-thirties, I decided to mail letters to each of those families and let them know what their support meant to me. I shared what I now know about my dad, the family disease of alcoholism, and how it affected me. They simply responded to me with compassion and said, *"We know. We knew then, but there was nothing we could do about it."* I hate to break it to you, but people know. It's sad and amusing how I thought no one knew when I was younger, but I barely understood what was happening myself. As a mother now, I know. I know when something feels off to me about a family and I keep my child away from them. Whether they say it to you, they know. Alternatively, at best, they suspect. If this is part of what is holding you back, don't use it as an excuse.

What if they take me out of my home? As hard as it is to hear, being removed from your home may be necessary. If you are experiencing physical, sexual, or emotional abuse, you do NOT deserve to be treated this way. I know it's scary to think about, but you are entitled to a safe, loving home. A place where someone loves, respects, and takes care of **you**. If your home is unstable or violent, this may be the best option for you. If you're uncomfortable talking about what is happening in person, there are online resources you can start with, which I list in the next chapter.

Maybe it Will Get Better?

When you're dealing with alcoholism or any kind of untreated addiction, things usually get worse. Like any disease, it progresses. Awareness is the first step, but action is critical. This means that knowing there is a problem isn't enough; you must get help to heal. Don't wait for your parents to figure out something is wrong and be there for you. Remember, unless they get support, they are not able to. It's up to you to find the right resources to start healing yourself —and my goal is to help you by writing this book.

The good news is when you do get help, things *can* get better, including your relationships with yourself, others, and your parents. When I started attending Al-Anon regularly in my mid to late twenties, my relationship with my dad improved. As I got better, he got better (a message you'll hear repeated in Al-Anon. He was there for many key moments, such as: attending both my college graduations, helping me move a few times after college, and teaching me how to fix things when I bought my first home. To his credit, he never accepted praise for my successes. He always says, *"She did it all by herself"* or *"I wasn't there for her."*

Additionally, my relationship with my mother has shifted since the birth of my child. She is a giving grandmother and at one point said to me, *"I have a lot to make up for with you."* I was speechless when she said this to me, but it started our healing journey. Her priority is and always will be my dad. As a mother, I struggle to understand this. However, she doesn't have the resources and tools I do. And you know what? Even with Google, friends who are fantastic mothers, therapists, a stable job, a safe home, and wonderful medications, being a parent is hard work. Really hard. I can't imagine what it was like for my parents living in alcoholism and not having any of these things.

As I continue to heal, I have remembered some good memories with my family. We took a lot of fun trips in the car, playing games. One summer, we watched every Clint Eastwood movie there was (and made funny voices as a family, using catchphrases). Each Christmas, we decorated the tree and I loved falling asleep under it at night, looking at the beautiful lights. I also enjoyed playing card games with my mom and building forts with my brother. I feel blessed to be able to see this now and accept it for what it was: the best my parents could do. Even if you don't experience these changes in your relationships with your family or others, you will still see a change in yourself, and that is worth more than anything.

I know getting help may seem overwhelming and impossible to manage, but the most important thing is that you start somewhere. One of my favorite quotes is by Lao Tzu: *"The journey of a thousand miles begins with one step."* It was the thousand little steps I took, sometimes inch-by-inch, that got me here. Buying this book, believe it or not, was your first step. Next, maybe you keep reading and learning about alcoholism. Then, maybe you go to a meeting in-person or online, whatever you think you can manage. Anything you do to take care of yourself, big or small, will get you closer to where you want to be.

While I don't know you personally, what I do know is this: You are smart enough to realize something is wrong. You are strong enough to seek help. This tells me you are brave enough to do whatever you need to get through this.

Thoughts to Consider:

1. How does reaching out for help make you feel? What could happen if you did?

2. What level of abuse are you experiencing in your home, if any?

3. Have you ever considered that you don't deserve to be abused, in any way? If so, what could you do to get help?

   If not, what one thing can you do to get help, and work toward achieving a sense of self-worth, love, and respect?

VII

Where Can You Get Help?

Below are some places you can get support safely and confidentially, both virtually and in-person. In our technology-driven world, there are more online resources available than ever before, making reaching out easier and anonymous. Educating yourself is also important; learning more about alcoholism and how it affects families will go a long way in managing this, now and in the future. If nothing below resonates with you, you can just Google "adult children of alcoholics" or "child of an alcoholic" to search for other resources. What's important is you find something, anything, to help you. You have been through enough already; let someone else help you through your pain.

Online / Face-to-Face Meetings

The Al-Anon Family Groups (AFG) offer a variety of support groups for those affected by someone's drinking. The primary purpose of these groups is to learn how to take care of yourself, not how to get the alcoholic to stop drinking. If you are between 10-20 years old (depending on your area's guidelines), you attend Alateen, which is focused on young children/relatives of alcoholics. Parents are not invited to Alateen, which gives members a safe space to share what they need to and learn from each other. After Alateen, you graduate to Al-Anon, which is for anyone impacted by someone's drinking. In every meeting, you will be given tools and resources to navigate this family disease.

Before you attend a meeting, online or in-person, you may find it helpful to listen to a few podcasts on how the program works: *First Steps to Al-Anon Recovery* (https://al-anon.org/newcomers/first-steps-al-anon-recovery/). At each meeting, the facilitator will ask if there are any newcomers. If so, someone in the group will give the newcomer welcome, which provides a brief overview of how the program works. Here is what I usually say:

> *"We welcome you to our program. We hope you will find the peace and healing that many of us have found. When we first came into Al-Anon, many of us were looking for ways to get the problem drinker in our lives to stop drinking. But this is a program for us. We learn how to put the focus on ourselves and take care of us, not to change the alcoholic. We focus on the three C's: we didn't cause alcoholism, we can't control it, and we can't cure it, but we can contribute to it through our actions.*
>
> *We suggest you try at least six different meetings before you decide whether this program is for you. Each meeting has a different flavor and style, so you may find one that speaks to you more than another. Our program is a spiritual one, not a religious one. You will hear mention of God or Higher Power. A higher power is something greater than yourself. It can be nature, God, or the group itself, but it is up to you how to define it. In fact, not all of us believe in God.*
>
> *Our meetings are confidential. What you see here, when you leave here, let it stay here. If we see you on the street, we may not speak to you. We do not want to risk the anonymity or safety of our members by exposing how we know each other, in other words, through Al-Anon. This is also why we introduce ourselves by first name only.*

As we share in the group, you will notice that we do not crosstalk. This means we do not comment directly on what anyone has said. We share our own experience, strength, and hope and let you 'take what you like and leave the rest.' If you want to speak to anyone after the meeting regarding something you heard, please do so."

The Al-Anon program is based on the 12 Steps of Alcoholics Anonymous. This is called "working the steps" which is how you get through recovery. In time, you should get a sponsor. A sponsor is someone who guides you through the program and works the steps with you. Ideally, you choose a sponsor by listening to people share in the group and find someone you feel comfortable with. It's okay to switch sponsors if you need to. I've had a few sponsors in the program and each of them added value to my recovery.

Below, please find some links to access Al-Anon meetings, literature, and other useful resources.

Al-Anon Family Groups (includes Alateen):

- Al-Anon Web site: https://Al-Anon.org
- Al-Anon Meetings (in-person and online): https://Al-Anon.org/Al-Anon-meetings/find-an-Al-Anon-meeting/ or call 1-888-425-2666
- Al-Anon Meetings (online): https://al-anon.org/al-anon-meetings/electronic-meetings/
- Al-Anon Family Group Headquarters
  Phone: 1-757-563-1600
  Email: wso@Al-Anon.org
  Address: 1600 Corporate Landing Parkway Virginia Beach, VA 23454-5617

Alateen *(found on Al-Anon's home page: https://Al-Anon.org)*
- Alateen Meetings (in-person): Under **Find a Meeting**, select **Find an Alateen Meeting**
- Alateen Meetings (online): Under **Newcomers**, select **Teen Corner (Alateen)**
  - This includes an online **Alateen Chat Meeting**

As I mentioned earlier, Adult Children of Alcoholics (ACOA) meetings. ACOA evolved into ACA, Adult Children of Alcoholics/Dysfunctional Families, and is now a program for children who grew up in dysfunctional homes. It focuses on growing up in an environment of abuse, neglect, and trauma and how it affects all aspects of our lives. ACA provides a safe space for us to grieve our childhoods and begin to heal. I found it beneficial to be in these meetings with other teenagers and adults like me. ACA meetings are not as easy to find as Al-Anon meetings, so if there is not an ACA meeting near you, you can attend Al-Anon. After I moved, I transitioned to Al-Anon and found it just as helpful.

Adult Children of Alcoholics / Dysfunctional Families (ACA):
- ACA Web site: https://adultchildren.org/
- ACA Meetings (in-person): https://adultchildren.org/meeting-search/
- ACA Meetings (online): ACA has Skype, Phone, and Internet Meetings you can access under **Resources**

I'm including AA because you can learn a lot by attending an open AA Meeting and listening to an AA speaker. It provides a different perspective of the disease, directly from someone who is in recovery.

Alcoholics Anonymous (AA):
- AA Web site: www.aa.org or https://aa-intergroup.org/
- AA Meetings: https://aa.org/pages/en_US/meeting-guide or https://aa-intergroup.org/oiaa/meetings/

- AA World Service Office
  Phone: 1-212-870-3400
  Address: 475 Riverside Drive at West 120th St., 11th Floor
  New York, NY 10115

Finally, I am adding a few resources for suicide prevention and domestic violence. If you are feeling suicidal and thinking of taking your life, or are living in an abusive environment, please reach out. Your life is worth it. **You** are worth it.

Suicide Prevention and Education:
- National Suicide Prevention Lifeline
  - Web site: https://suicidepreventionlifeline.org/
  - Phone: 1-800-273-TALK (8255)
- American Foundation for Suicide Prevention (AFSP): http://www.afsp.org/
- American Association of Suicidology (AAS): http://www.suicidology.org/
- Suicide Prevention Resource Center (SPRC): http://www.sprc.org/

Domestic Violence Support:
- National Domestic Violence Hotline
  - Web site: https://www.thehotline.org/
  - Phone: 1-800-799-7233
    (If you are afraid your Internet usage is being monitored, call the 800-number first.)
- National Coalition Against Domestic Violence (NCADV): https://ncadv.org/

RECOMMENDED READINGS:

The recommended books and literature below helped me learn a lot about alcoholism. I would start with Alateen and Al-Anon literature, as they are the most relatable and easiest to follow. Al-Anon's home page has a ton of reading materials (*https://Al-Anon.org*). If you cannot afford to purchase resources, contact the Al-Anon Family Group Headquarters by phone or mail and they can get you what you need for free or at a discounted rate.

- Go to Al-Anon's home page: *https://Al-Anon.org*
- Under **Members**, click **Member Resources**, then **Literature**. When you scroll down, there are lots of options, including **Free Downloadable Items**
- Under **Al-Anon Store**, scroll down on the right till you reach **Interest Categories** and search by category
- Some of my favorites include:
    - Alateen—A Day at a Time *(a daily reader with inspirational stories)*
    - Living Today in Alateen
    - Hope for Today *(specifically focused on adult children of alcoholics)*
    - One Day at a Time in Al-Anon
    - Courage to Change
    - How Al-Anon Works *(also available on Audible: https://www.audible.com/)*
    - Paths to Recovery

ACA's web site has valuable resources, specifically for adult children.

- Go to ACA's Website: https://adultchildren.org/
- At the top of the **Home Page**, select **Literature**; I recommend:
    - *Am I an Adult Child?* (https://adultchildren.org/newcomer/am-i-an-adult-child/)
        - ACA also has 25 questions to determine if you grew up in a dysfunctional home.
    - *The Laundry List* (https://adultchildren.org/literature/laundry-list/)
        - ACA has a list of 14 traits you can read to determine if you are affected by alcoholism or another addiction.
    - *The Problem* and *The Solution*

Magda's *Top 10 List of ACA Books* include:

- *Adult Children of Alcoholics* by Janet Geringer Woititz
- *The Complete ACOA Sourcebook: Adult Children of Alcoholics at Home, at Work, and in Love* by Janet Geringer Woititz
- *Perfect Daughters—Adult Daughters of Alcoholics* by Robert J. Ackerman
- *Silent Sons—A Book for and About Men* by Robert J. Ackerman
- *An Adult Child's Guide to What's "Normal"* by John Friel & Linda Friel (focuses on adult children of all addictions)
- *Codependent No More—How to Stop Controlling Others and Start Caring for Yourself* by Melody Beattie (focuses on being a codependent and healing from it)
- *Emotional Blackmail—When the People in Your Life Use Fear, Obligation, and Guilt to Manipulate You* by Susan Forward
- *Boundary Power: How I Treat You, How I Let You Treat Me, How I Treat Myself* by Mike S. O'Neil & Charles E. Newbold (I worked through this one with a therapist)
- *Guinevere Gets Sober,* by Jennifer Matesa (focuses on growing up in an alcoholic home): http://guineveregetssober.com/adult-children-of-alcoholics/

RESOURCES AT SCHOOL:

A great place to get help is your school, especially because you already spend so much time there and your parents likely won't question it. I mentioned most of these resources before, but as a quick reminder, here they are again:

- Guidance counselor/s
- Safe teacher/s
- Alateen meetings (if they are held at your school)

PERSONAL OUTLETS:

A personal outlet is anything you can do that brings you peace and freedom. A personal outlet should be healthy and *not* self-destructive. I know it may be tempting to engage in harmful behaviors, such as drugs or alcohol, but those will lead you down the same path as your alcoholic parent and continue the cycle you want to break. If you find yourself struggling with those habits already, it's that much more important for you to attend a support group or individual counseling. Please talk to someone! You can also replace those unhealthy coping mechanisms with one of the personal outlets below (or anything positive that is therapeutic for you).

- Writing/journaling
- Art (drawing or painting)
- Music (writing songs *or* listening to music)
- Exercise
- After-school programs (e.g. sports, drama, music, yearbook)
- Guided meditations, deep breathing, and visualization:
  - These are wonderful tools to ground and calm yourself when you are upset. You can learn more by searching Google, but here are a couple of my favorite guided meditations:
    - https://www.youtube.com/watch?v=4EaMJOo1jks&t=2s
    - https://www.youtube.com/watch?v=tW4rDPmFVkg
- Safe family members who you can trust, and could even take you in
- Friends, or your friends' parents, who you can trust, visit, or turn to for support

Depending on who you reach out to and their understanding of alcoholism, you may get some uneducated responses. As a teenager, a friend of mine went to her aunt for help. Her aunt simply said, "*Why don't you just tell your father to stop drinking?*" With all we know, some people still think this way. If you encounter someone like this, perhaps you can share this book with them, or another resource, to educate them on alcoholism and how it affects everyone involved. If that doesn't work, find someone who is compassionate and knowledgeable about addiction that can guide you to the right place.

Religious / Faith-Based Outlets:

If you are religious, you can speak to the pastor or other religious liaison at your local church, mosque, temple, etc. You can also access sermons and other inspirational messages online. Listening to Pastor Joel Osteen is healing for me. I listed a couple of his sermons that are meaningful to me, but as they say in Al-Anon, "*Take what you like and leave the rest.*"

- "*You are Not Damaged Goods*" by Joel Osteen: https://sermons.love/joel-osteen/3401-joel-osteen-you-are-not-damaged-goods.html
- An Interview with Tyler Perry: https://www.youtube.com/watch?v=TQtxmxxQjU0
  - Tyler grew up in an abusive home and when I listen to him speak, I believe I can make it through anything.
    - *Note*: This link seems to change, so if it doesn't work, Google "Joel Osteen interview with Tyler Perry" from October 24, 2018.

Private Counseling (Individual and Family):

Finally, as mentioned throughout this book, private counseling—individual and family—is another way for you to get help. If your family is aware of what is going on, you may want to talk to them about getting a counselor for yourself and/or for the whole family. The information you share with a counselor is confidential and talking to one gives you a safe space to express your feelings and get professional support. There is one exception to confidentiality: the laws in all 50 states require a therapist to contact authorities if a patient is a danger to him/herself, to others, and/or if the therapist suspects a child is being abused. While this may seem difficult to understand, it is not only for your safety but also for the safety of others. Here are two resources you can use to find private counseling:

Psychology Today: https://www.psychologytoday.com/us/therapists

- On the **Home Page,** enter your **Zip Code**
- Under **Interests** on the left-hand side menu, search for therapists who specialize in the following categories: Addiction, Alcohol Use, Child or Adolescent, Codependency, or Trauma and PTSD. Depending on the exact details of your family situation, a different category may be a better fit for you.
- Most therapists do a phone screen to figure out what is going on and how they can assist you. Ask them what types of counseling they provide and have them explain the process to you. Make sure to find somebody who you feel comfortable with so that you can make the most of your time with them. It's okay if you don't like someone—trust your gut! There are plenty of options out there.

Find a therapist online: https://www.e-counseling.com/tlp/find-therapist/

- Online therapy can be a good option if you cannot leave home; however, this may require insurance or your parents' approval if you are under 18. Read the reviews on each of the different providers and select one that seems like a good fit for you.

Keep in mind that once you reach out for help and start taking care of yourself, the alcoholic(s) in your life will likely push back. They don't want you to change, for various reasons. They might be afraid they are going to lose you, afraid you won't support them anymore, and/or are unsure of how to handle the new you. A professional can guide you through the best ways to deal with this, based on your circumstances.

> *"There is a crack in everything. That's how the light gets in."*
> —*Leonard Cohen*

Without challenges in life, we would never grow. As you begin to heal, your sense of self-reliance will grow and your ability to persist will become stronger because you won the battle, big or small. Surviving this will increase your faith in whatever higher power you believe in. Once you learn what you can achieve, you can dream bigger dreams, and do whatever you put your mind to. When I look back at what I've made it through, I know I can accomplish anything.

Thoughts to Consider:
1. What resource/s can you try now?

2. What resource/s can you take advantage of later?

WHERE CAN YOU GET HELP?

3. List the next step you will take on your healing journey (like visiting a website listed above). Remember, every one counts!

VIII

It Does Get Better

"The world breaks everyone, and afterward, many are stronger at the broken places." —Ernest Hemingway

After all is said and done, where am I today, as I write the final chapter of this book?

Healing.

That's the best word I can use to describe it. I'm stronger, wiser, happier, and more fulfilled than I've ever been. Hemingway's quote above captures my journey well. The truth is I continue to manage the effects of growing up in an alcoholic household, more than 20 years after leaving it. I won't sugarcoat it for you because that's not who I am. I am still capable of repeating the same cycle of abuse and finding toxic people to put into any area of my life. Because of my Al-Anonism, I now know I cannot be in a relationship with an alcoholic, addict, or codependent; it will trigger <u>my</u> codependency. Most importantly, I don't want to be in those kinds of relationships anymore. I deserve love and respect and I won't settle for anything less, in any relationship.

It's taken me a long time to believe it, but today I know I have worth. I just need to be me—nothing more, nothing less. I am learning to live in peace—to be happy, quiet, and still. My biggest challenge remains using my voice and speaking up, but I have made tremendous strides with this. These are skills I acquired in Al-Anon, therapy, and other healing practices, and yes, I still work on them. In fact, I plan to work on them my entire life to be the best version of myself, not only for me but also for my child.

I wrote this book because I want to save you the years—heck, decades—it took me to understand how deeply this family disease penetrates. The sooner you know what is going on, the sooner you can get help and start living the abundant, healthy, happy life you deserve. Yes, you deserve to be happy. You deserve respect and love. And you don't need anyone to give it to you…you already have it within.

Gratitude, Despite the Pain

One of Al-Anon's key principles is an attitude of gratitude. There is always something to be grateful for in a day, in a situation, or in a person. There is something called the 21 Day Gratitude Challenge. The goal is to write down at least 3–5 things every day for 21 days that you are grateful for. It can be as simple as the sun rising, the clothes you're wearing, or your health, but try to find something new each day. If you do this for 21 days straight, your perspective on life and your situation will shift for the better.

My sponsor once told me that our greatest teachers in life are sometimes the most difficult. Life lessons are not pretty, wrapped in a box and tied with a bow. I think this is one of the blessings in having my parents (some days, I need to remind myself of that more than others). It took me a long time and a lot of work in Al-Anon to see the good I inherited from them.

My father taught me to take care of everything I own. He showed me how to maintain my car and fix things around the house, something I take pride in as a woman. My mother taught me how to be kind, how to smile, and how to be resourceful. I have both my parents' work ethic. They are hard workers dedicated to their jobs (unless the disease gets in the way). My parents also have giving natures, especially when it comes to those struggling or in need. This impacted me and encouraged my volunteerism and community involvement.

It also took me a long time to see the *not so good* I inherited from my parents. Though we fight it, we can take on the negative traits of our parents if we are not vigilant. I was angry about this for a while (*it's their fault I have these issues*), but if you hold on to anger and resentment toward them, it will affect you. An Al-Anon quote states, *"Resentment is a poison you drink and hope the other person dies."* This is where doing the work helps you let go of the anger and hurt.

As a Christian, one of the primary principles of my faith is love. Everyone deserves love. We are all children of God, formed in His image, including my parents. They are on their own journey, their own path, with whatever life lessons they must learn. My job is not to condemn, judge, or persecute them. My job is to send them love and compassion. Sadly, my parents don't know what unconditional love is. They haven't experienced it in their lives. I am blessed to know that love through Al-Anon, my friends, and God. Even if it's only for a day here and there, I can show my parents unconditional love. Sometimes you have to do this from afar, and that's okay. But I find coming from this place gives me more peace than living in anger and resentment.

I'm not saying that you shouldn't allow yourself to feel whatever emotions you have from your childhood: grief, anger, sadness, rejection, or something else. Feel, **and then** get to a better place. A place where you can forgive your parents for what they've done, no matter how wrong, because you understand "they know not what they do." Make your love stronger than hate.

My Prayer for You

My hope and prayer for you is this: That you get to where I am—this beautiful, healing, serene place. I know it feels like it will never end, and you can't see the light, but I promise you there is an end to the darkness. I believe we all have potential; a greatness inside of us to discover, a fire burning brightly. Other people tried to put out my flame, not only my parents. As I got older, I realized they may have felt threatened, confused, or intimidated by me. My fire got down to an ember at times, but that ember survived. Today, it burns brighter and stronger than I ever. Don't let anyone put out your fire; instead, let it light up the darkness!

The last words I will say to encourage you are these: Put the focus on yourself. Remember, you cannot change the alcoholic or get them to stop drinking. Only they can change, if they choose to. What you *can* control is yourself. You can control how you respond and react to things. You can change any of the behaviors that don't serve you. But to do this, you must remain open to healing.

If you still feel none of this applies to you, that's okay. Keep this book as a resource for later in your life. Maybe you'll start to see some of the patterns I described once you get older, and something will click. This book will always be here for you. I will always be here for you. Maybe you read this book, see yourself clearly in it, and you want to get help. I am here cheering you on. **You can do it!**

Whatever your situation, don't forget I'm praying for you. Someone who doesn't know you sees who you are and appreciates the potential inside of you. I went through hell and I more than survived it, I made a great life. And you know what? It gets better each day, and I'm excited to see what's next! My daughter and I have a beautiful, safe space to call home, where she can be exactly who God intended her to be, with parents who love and encourage her. What a blessing that I can give her what I didn't have as a child. If I can end this cycle, I know you can, too. Be a chain breaker! It stops with *you*.

Thoughts to Consider:

1. How do you feel after reading this book?

2. Do you think your family may be suffering from the family disease of alcoholism? If so, are you open to getting help?

3. What "next" step are you going to take? (Yes, I'm asking you again!)

References

I. Is This Normal?

1. "Has Your Life Been Affected by Someone's Drinking? Al-Anon Family Groups, https://Al-Anon.org/newcomers/self-quiz/, Al-Anon Family Group Headquarters, Inc. (accessed 18 May 2019)

II. What Does it All Mean?

2. Alcoholics Anonymous (Fourth Edition, 2001). *The Doctor's Opinion* (pp. xxvii). Alcoholics Anonymous World Services, Inc.
3. "The Alcoholic Allergy." Ventura Recovery Center. Copyright © 2020 Ventura Recovery Center Drug and Alcohol Addiction Treatment. https://venturarecoverycenter.com/alcoholic-allergy/ (accessed 21 June 2020).
4. Thomas, Scot, MD, "Wet Brain from Alcohol: Signs, Symptoms, and Recovery," *American Addiction Centers,* Copyright American Addiction Centers, https://americanaddictioncenters.org/alcoholism-treatment/wet-brain (accessed 29 March 2019).
5. "Co-Dependency," *Mental Health America*, Copyright Mental Health America, http://www.mentalhealthamerica.net/co-dependency (accessed 10 April 2019).
6. "Genetics of Alcoholism," *Addiction Center,* https://www.addictioncenter.com/alcohol/genetics-of-alcoholism/ (accessed 21 June 2020).

V. How I Survived

7. Harris, Ed. *To Everything There is a Season*, http://www.godsongs.net/2016/07/to-everything-there-is-season-ed-harris.html (accessed 21 June 2020).